Nanna's Colouring Book...
...and mine too!

Volume 3

I ♡ colouring with Nanna

Janet McCormick

Colouring Tips

If you place a blank sheet of paper behind the page
you are about to colour, this will ensure
the following page is protected from any marks.

The last pages in the book are blank,
so you can take them out to use as
blotting sheets or colour test pages.

The designs are printed on one side only,
and there are wide margins,
so pages can be cut out for colouring,
or for display and framing.

Older kids can use a fine line black marker
to add more intricate patterns into the
simpler designs if they like.

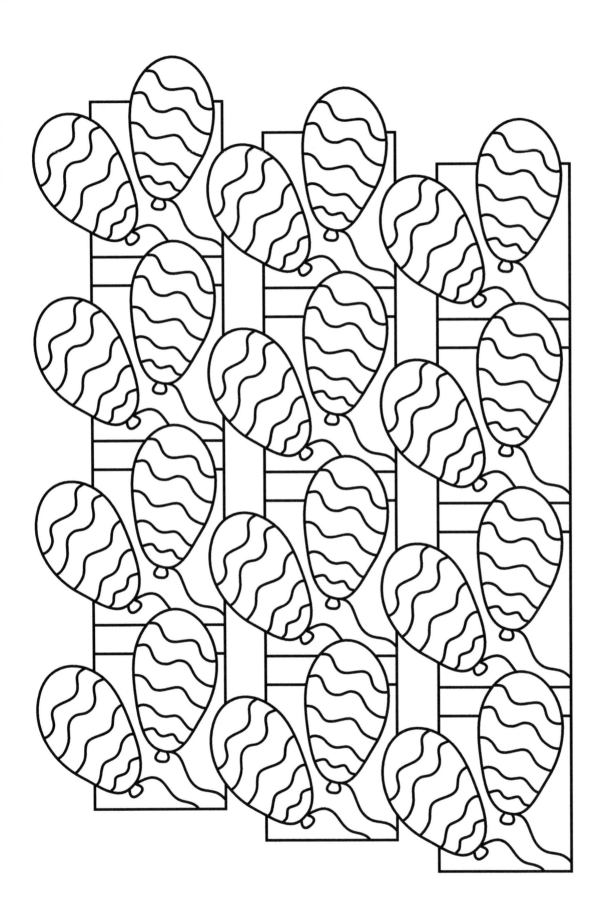

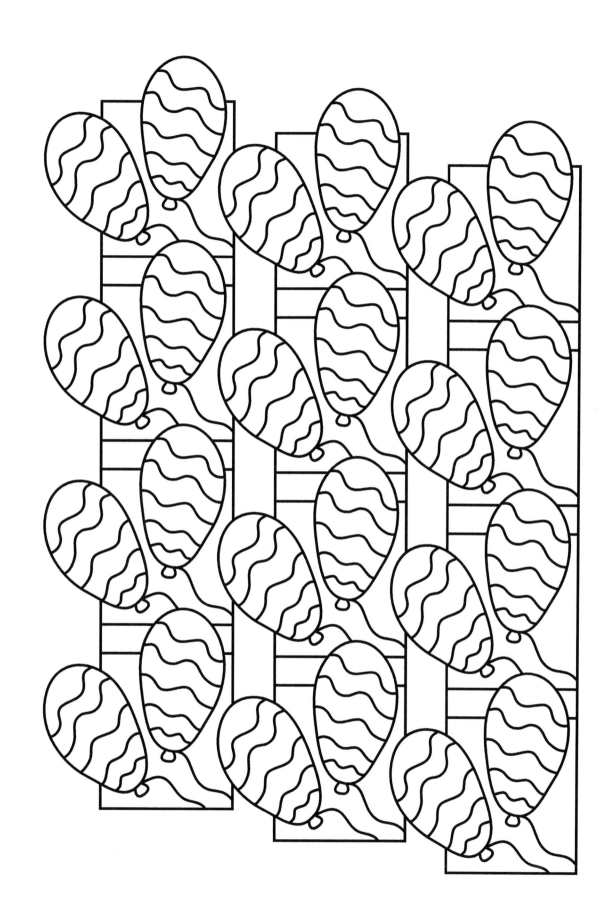

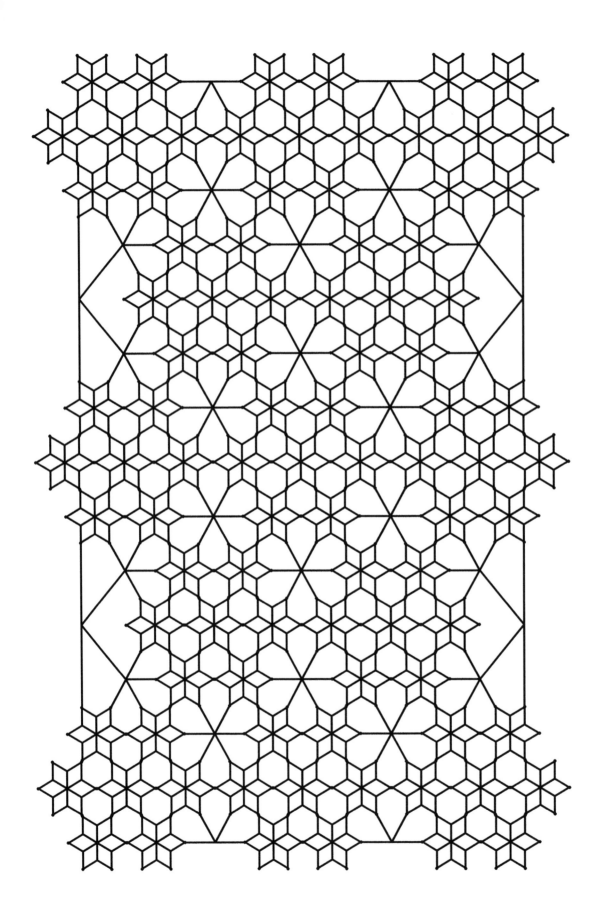

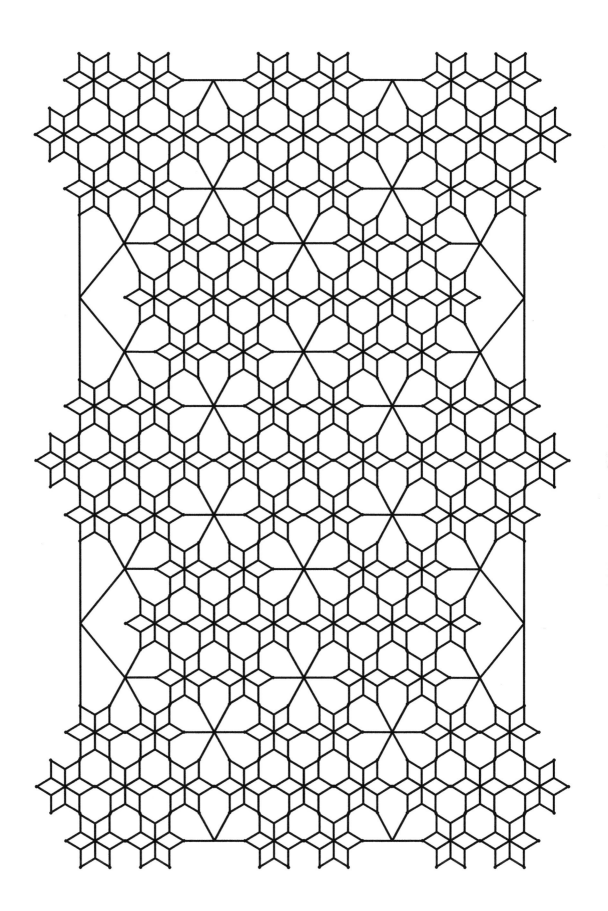

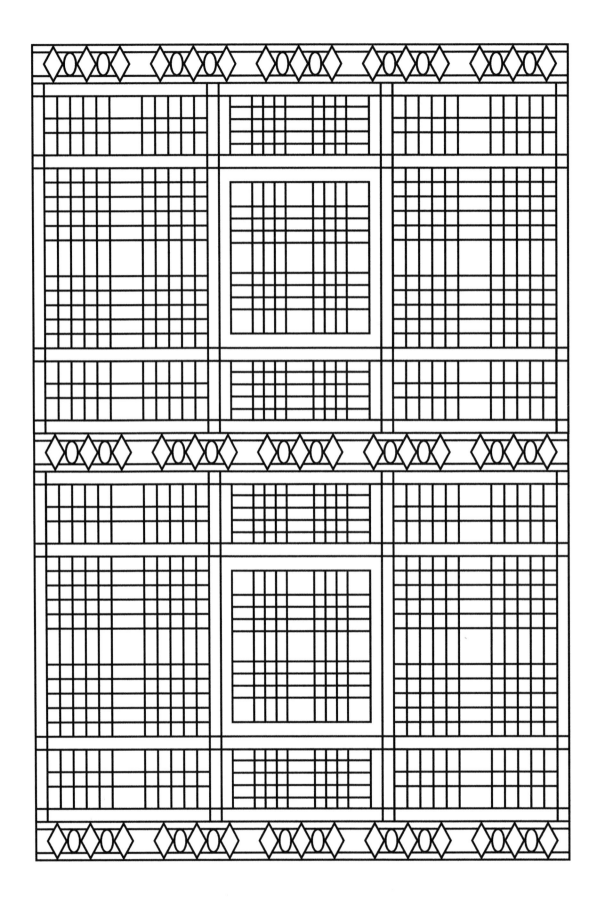

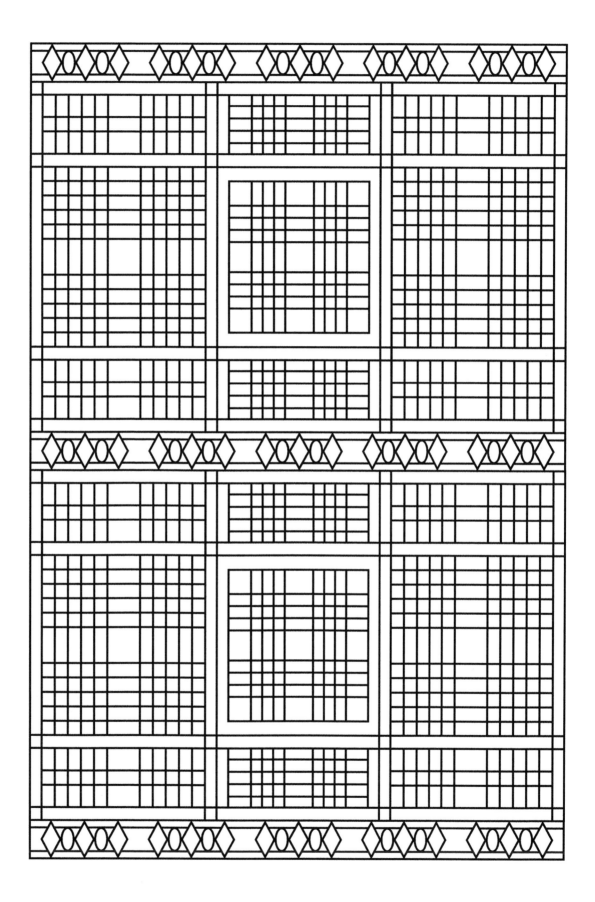

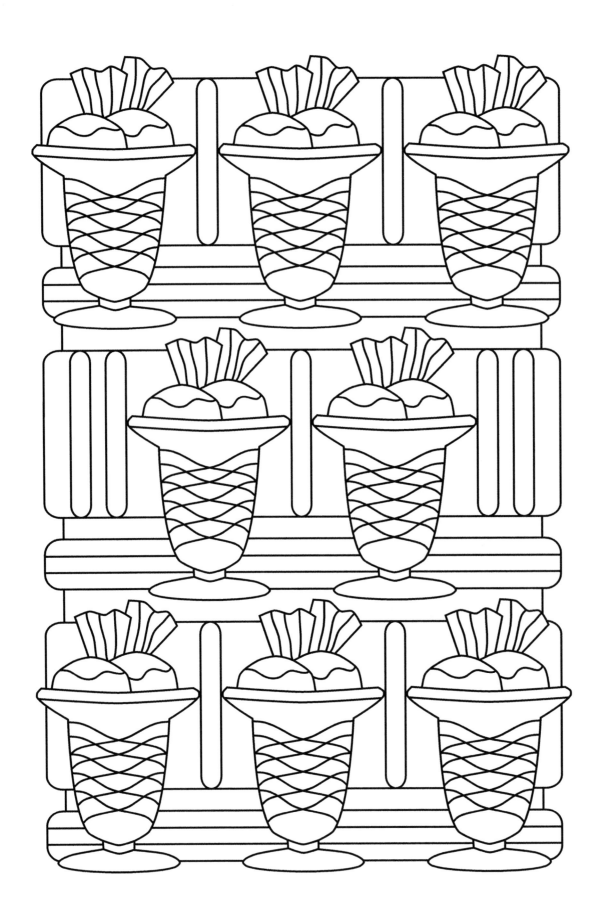

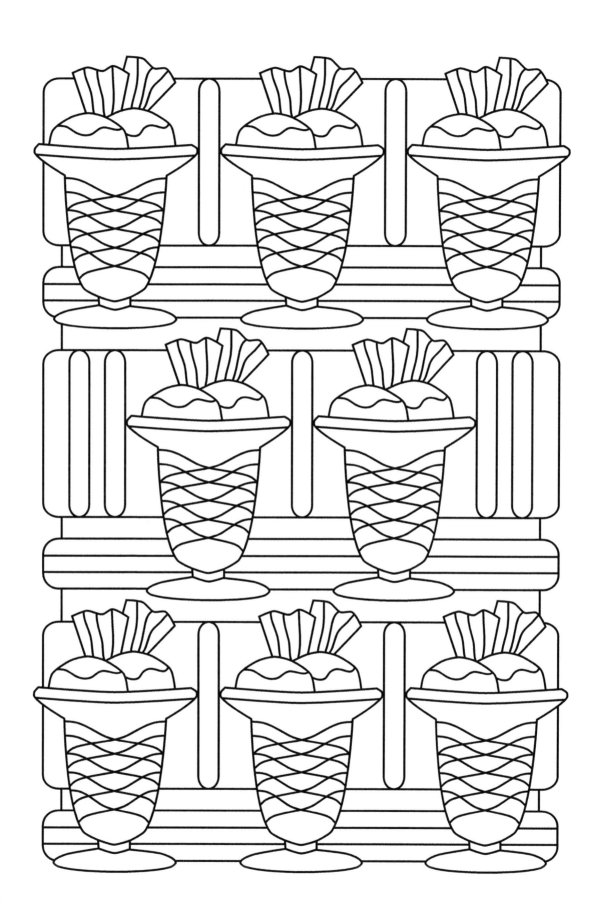

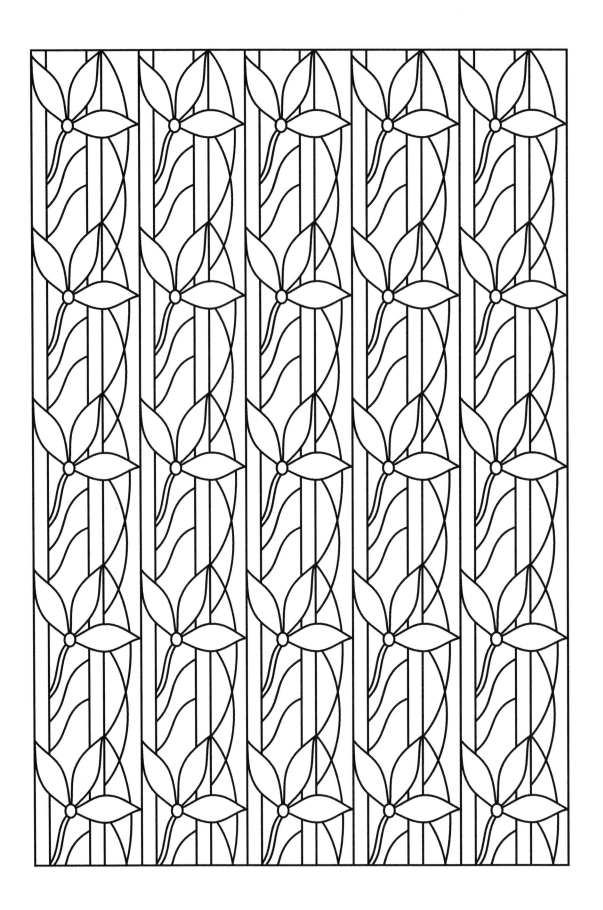

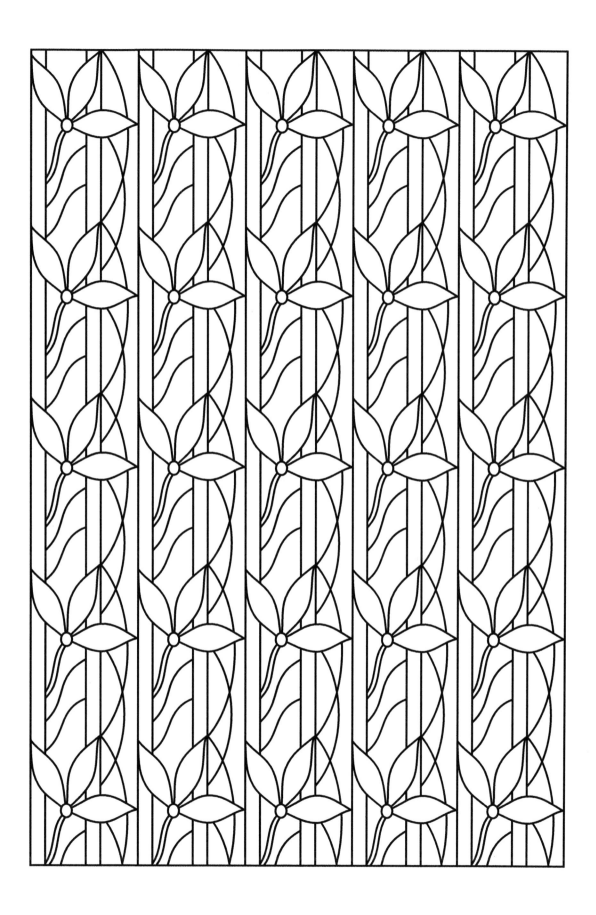

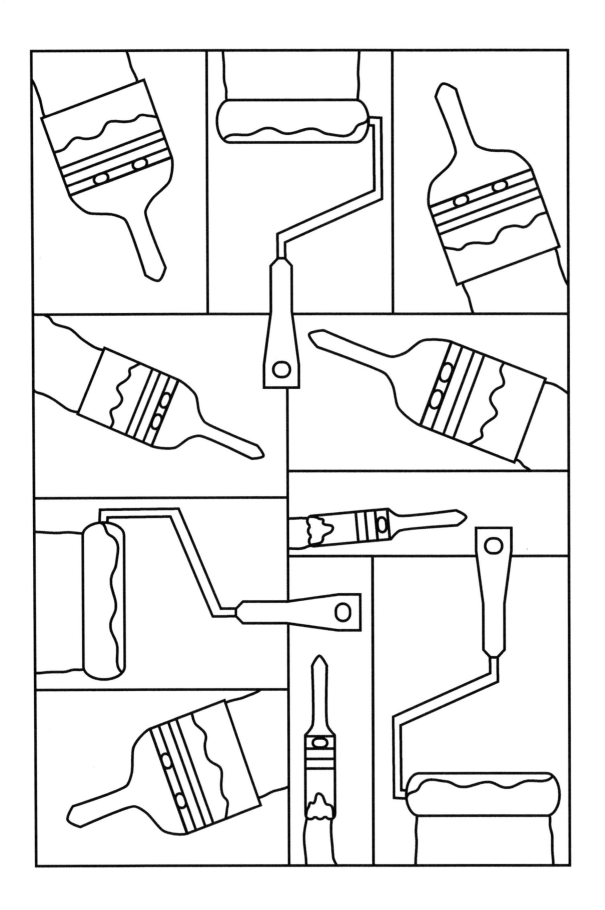

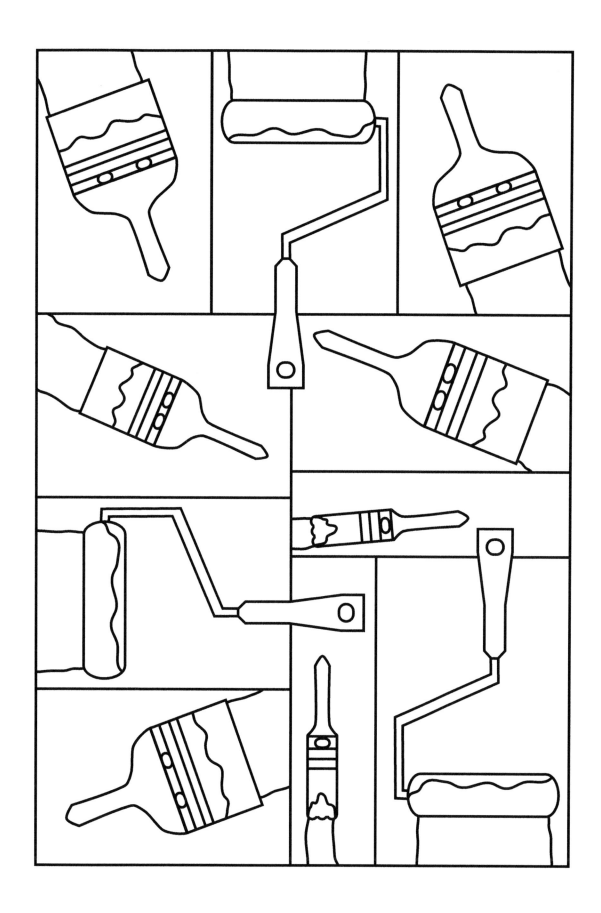

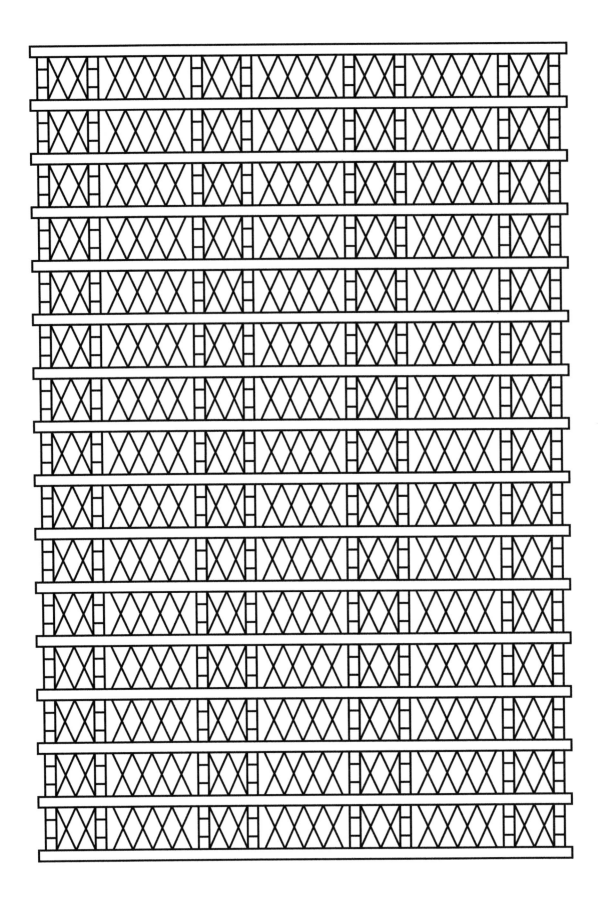

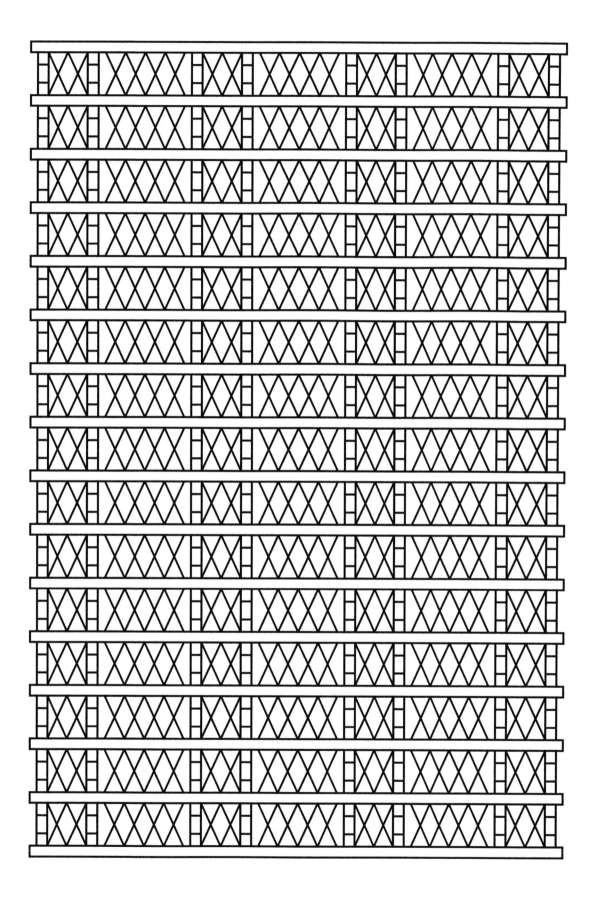

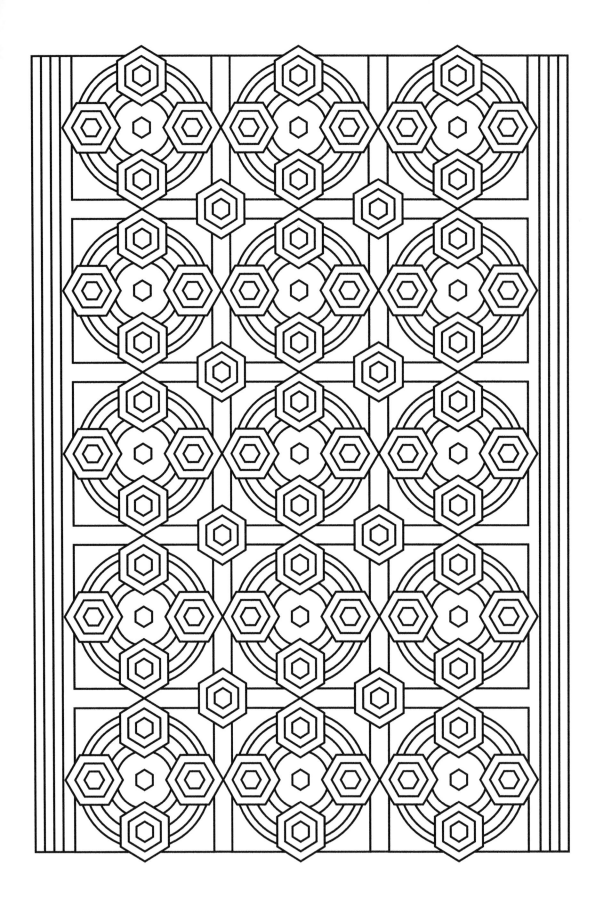

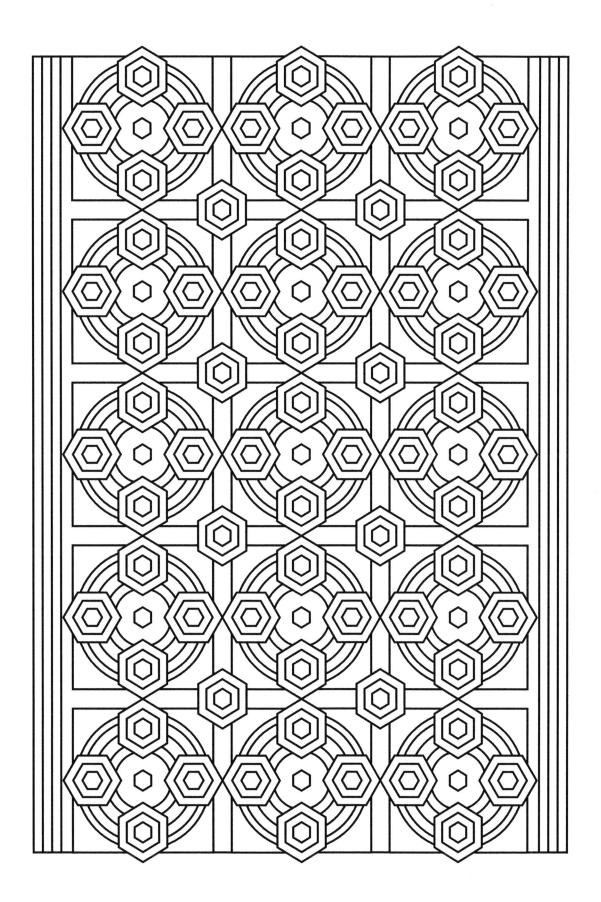

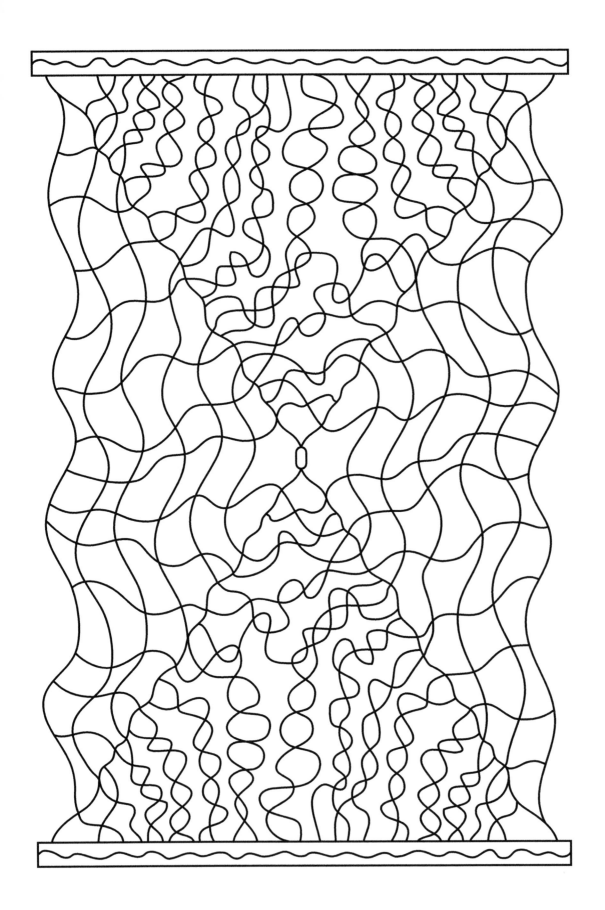

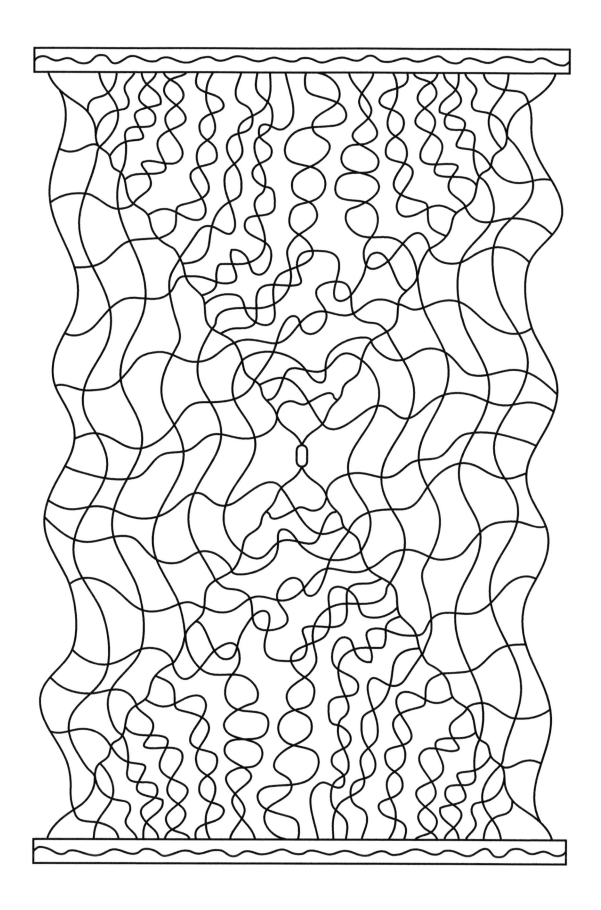

Blotting Sheets or Colour Test Pages